Blogging for Profit:

The Ultimate Beginners Guide to Learn Step-by-Step How to Make Money Blogging and Earn Passive Income up to $10,000 a Month

Daren H. Russell

Table of Contents

What This Book Will Teach You

Are you curious to learn about Blogging for Passive Income but unsure where to start?

Have you always wanted to make money from Blogging, but are intimidated by the technical jargon being used?

If these questions relate well with you, then this book is for you. In this book you will find the basic essentials to learning Blogging. This book introduces readers to blogging, the in's and out, the various processes and steps involved in it.

Who this Book is for

This book contains information on how to learn Blogging from a beginner level.

Readers who can benefit the most from the book include:

- Professionals who would like to know more about the Blogging as an income replacement so they can quit their 9-to-5 job.

- Writers interested in earning money from Blogging

- Entrepreneurs who want to learn Blogging as another possible source of income

How this Book is Organized

This book is organized into three parts. The parts are best read in chronological order. Once you become familiar with all the steps outlined in the book, you can go directly to the techniques which apply to your current situation the best.

The three parts of the book are:

Part One outlines the essential topics on Blogging, and then making money from Blogging in particular. The section also talks about how important it is to learn these topics as a beginner in order to form a solid foundation in doing the right steps – from introductory concepts to making your first Blog post.

Part Two is about the Blogging in more detail. You'll learn how to write your very first Blog post, manage and schedule your blog content and how to implement the steps discussed.

Part Three discusses more in-depth topics on Blogging such as:

- Promoting your Blog

- Scaling Up your Blog Profit – up to $10,000 a month

- Plus, a BONUS Chapter on Integrating Social Media

Introduction:

Congratulations on owning *Blogging for Profit: The Ultimate Beginners Guide to Learn Step-by-Step How to Make Money Blogging and Earn Passive Income up to $10,000 a Month,* and thank you for doing so. You have taken the first step into the world of blogging. It can be scary at first with the knowledge that complex technologies and complicated software stand in the way of achieving your goals. Don't panic. In a few easy steps, this book will walk you through everything you will need to know about how to start your blog, choose a subject to write about, get the word out, and start making money at the click of a button. Pretty soon, you will be on your way to a potentially lucrative job.

The following chapters will discuss blogging as a business. We will begin with the basics: what a blog is, what a blogger does, and how even a technology novice can make money with a blog. We will walk through the steps of creating a blog from concept to completion. Then, most importantly, we will discuss strategies that you can use to earn up to $10,000 a month with your blog.

In each chapter, you will find accessible information aimed at getting you started on your first blog. Each chapter includes easy-to-follow instructions and bullet points, and concludes with a step-by-step tutorial so that you can put what you have just learned into action!

There are plenty of books on this subject on the market. Thanks again for choosing this one! Every effort was made to ensure it is full of as much useful information as possible so please enjoy!

Chapter 1: What is Blogging and How Can It Make You Money?

Chapter 1: What is Blogging and How Can It Make You Money?

So what is a blog anyway? How is it different from a website?

First of all, blogs are different from websites. Websites are static pages on the Internet that host information, photographs, and other media. Wikipedia and Facebook are examples of websites. Blogs, short for weblogs, consist of a collection of posts. Good blogs are constantly updating and changing. In short, a blog is a journal (log) on the web. Some of the most popular blogs out there include the Huffington Post, TechCrunch, Lifehacker, and Mashable.

Blogs are almost as old as the Web itself.

As a platform for self-publishing, blogs first became popular in the late 1990s. The blogosphere exploded in the 2000's with the arrival of online newspapers like the Huffington Post and online magazines like *Wired*. Today it is a phenomenon that can't be stopped. The blogosphere is growing bigger every day. There are nearly 200 million blogs on the internet today, and over 1 million posts are published every day.

In addition to the growing size of the blogosphere itself, blogs are increasingly being used to make money. Making money from blogging isn't like e-commerce. Websites like Amazon and Walmart.com connect customers with products. Customers log onto these sites, shop for goods, and pay electronically. Then their order is either mailed to their door or is set aside at a physical store for the customer to pick up later. We'll get into the mechanics of how to monetize blogs in later chapters.

This may seem counterintuitive, but blogs don't actually sell tangible products; your commodity is information. Bloggers write posts or entries on the site. Think of it as something like a passage in a diary or a journal.

Belonging to an Affiliate marketing program, also called pay-per-click advertising, blogs can generate thousands of dollars a month. In brief, a company will pay you a small commission when a visitor clicks on an ad displayed on your site. Those clicks add up quickly if you run a popular blog with high traffic.

In several rare cases, blog behemoths rake in millions of dollars a month. That's million with an M. According to *Forbes*, Arianna Huffington of The Huffington Post generates an average of $14,000,000 a month from sponsored advertising. Mario Armando Lavandeira Jr. draws a monthly income of $575,000 in advertising revenue from his gossip website (PerezHilton.com). Peter Rojas' Gizmodo, an online magazine that features articles about design and technology, earns$ 352,000 a month from clickable ads.

Every successful blogger starts from scratch. It helps to visualize that, a decade or more ago, Huffington, Lavandeira, and Rojas were in your shoes. That being said, the novice blogger doesn't make it to fame and fortune overnight. Developing a successful and lucrative blog takes time, effort, patience, and determination.

As you walk down the path to becoming a successful blogger, it may feel like you're taking baby steps, just like pay-per-click advertising generates pennies. But hang in there, because one day in the near future, you will need to get a bigger piggy bank. By following the steps in this book, you can begin earning right away. If you are patient, eventually those pennies will add up to $10,000 a month.

Now that you have discarded any preconceived notions about making millions overnight, let me clarify why blogging requires patience and determination. Becoming a successful blogger requires a shift in mindset. It might look easy, but monetizing your blog demands a business-like attitude. Lots of bloggers are mere hobbyists, and in some rare cases, the casual blogger can become a success. Lucrative blogs entail the regular update of content, consistently scheduled posts, and an intelligent marketing strategy.

When you shift your mindset from one of the casual hobbyists to the determined businessperson, you should be able to see the myriad benefits. In the next chapter, we will begin to explore what should be the look and feel of the content of your blog. Then, we will walk through the software and strategies you will be using to create your blog from scratch! Deciding to dive into the deep end can seem scary at first, but only then can you enjoy the water.

Here's a quick overview of the journey

we are about to take:

- First, you will choose a topic for your blog. This will entail brainstorming what type of audience you will be addressing.
- Then, we will explore several ways to monetize your blog.
- Chapters 4, 5, and 6 lead you through the technical stuff. You will learn how to use the software on one of the most popular blogging platforms (Wordpress.com).
- Chapter 7 provides a crash course in Affiliate marketing. It will familiarize you with the technical process of how the model works as well as how to set up your blog with pay-per-click ads so that you can start making money!

- In the final chapters, we will learn about how to draw traffic to your blog using search engine optimization (SEO).
- Finally, we will look at your long-term goals.

CHAPTER SUMMARY:

1. In this chapter, we learned about blogs, the history of blogging, and some of the world's most successful bloggers.
2. We walked through some of the basics of what it takes to monetize a blog.
3. You learned about the important shift in mindset to become a successful blogger.

YOUR QUICK START ACTION STEP:

1. Let's begin with a warm-up exercise. Browse one or more of these blogs, all of which draw in more than $100,000 a month.

    a. The Huffington Post (www.huffingtonpost.com)

    b. Engadget (www.engadget.com)

    c. Moz (www.moz.com)

    d. Mashable (www.mashable.com)

    e. Techcrunch (www.techcrunch.com)

    f. Perez Hilton (www.perezhilton.com)

    g. Gizmodo (www.gizmodo.com)

h. Smashing Magazine (www.smashingmagazine.com)

2. Take notes. Does the look and feel of the blog align with the content? How is the site laid out? How frequently are posts published? What types of ads do you see, and where are they located on the page?

3. By following these initial steps, you will begin to recognize what design and content choices go into making a great blog. It will also help you to begin thinking about the design and content of your own blog.

Chapter 2: Discovering Your Niche

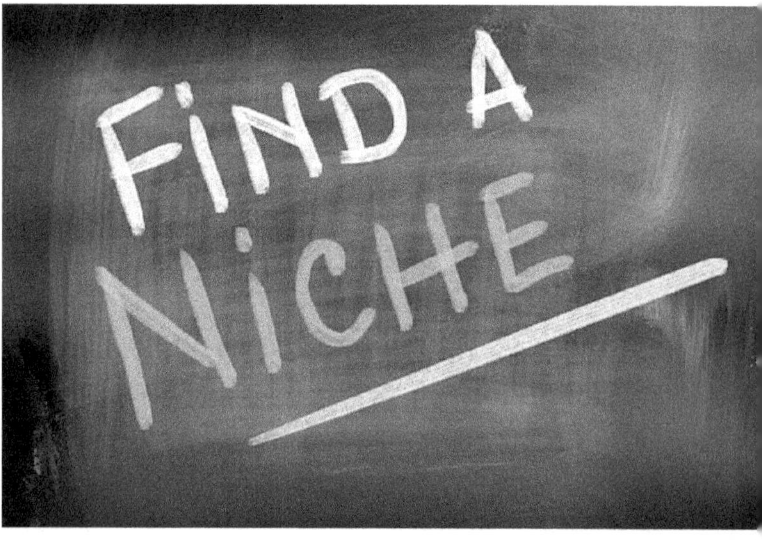
FIND A
NICHE

Chapter 2: Discovering Your Niche

So what kind of blogger are you? Blogs generally take several forms. Confessional bloggers post about personal experience or advice. DIY bloggers write about how to make things. The expert blogger or aspiring enthusiast provides information about a specialized subject. The savvy business person will likely blog about current events or strategies from the corporate world.

So how do you go about deciding on your topic? The answer to this question will have to do not only with what type of information you want to convey to your audience but with what form of writing that comes most naturally to you. Do you write in a personal style?

Are you a list maker? Or perhaps you are a practical-minded doer.

There are several factors to consider. How big is your audience? A blog about kayaking will be more successful than a blog about Neolithic Middle Eastern basket weaving; that's just basic math. There are more people online looking for information about outdoor recreation than those interested in Neolithic Middle Eastern basket weaving. In the first place, water sports is a broad subject, so it is unlikely that you will run out of material to write about. Secondly, how many internet browsers do you think are out there looking to learn how to craft using obscure, ancient techniques?

Now, let's do a little brainstorming. Choose a category from the list below.

Then we'll hone it down to get to a general subject. Lastly, we'll settle on a topic that is specific, but not too specific.

- Automotive
- Fashion and Beauty
- Food and Nutrition
- Technology and Electronics
- Fitness and Health
- Arts and Crafts
- Music
- Sports
- Nature

Some of the most popular blogs out there include recipes for cooks, travelogues, product reviews, troubleshooting guides, or comprehensive guides.

When choosing a topic for your blog, consider what you are passionate about.

Writing about a topic that inspires your creativity will help keep you motivated to post new articles on your blog. It will also help to attract readers because when you are passionate about the subject of your blog, your writing will naturally improve. Your passion will come through in your writing.

For instance, if fly fishing is your favorite hobby, your first-hand experience and expertise will also be an asset when you go about writing up your posts. You will already be an expert on that topic, and your readers will expect you to be knowledgeable about your topic.

Key benefits of defining the niche that's right for you include:

- Your writing will come across with passion and exuberance.
- You will probably already be knowledgeable on the topic.
- Your focused topic will attract a particular target audience.
- Your focused topic will give your blog a unique identity.

Here is a list of some popular niches that bloggers have chosen in the past:

- Car repair hacks
- Beauty and/or fashion tips
- Paleo cooking and recipes
- Product reviews of computers, laptops, and tablets
- Best yoga techniques
- Instructions and designs for DIY home decor
- Going green (Sustainability)

Once you have chosen a topic, you will be one step closer to discovering your niche.

1. Begin by identifying your topic from the list above.
2. What about this topic are you passionate about?
3. What aspect of this topic are you most knowledgeable about?
4. Make a list of up to a dozen niche ideas.
5. Cross off the items that are too broad or too specific.
6. Cross off the items that have little to no profitability. A niche will be profitable if it relates either directly or indirectly with a saleable product or service.

Example Site

Over the next few chapters, we will construct the foundation for your first blog. Our example niche will be yoga. Our sub-niche will be an audience interested in learning more about holistic lifestyles and mindful meditation. So do you see how choosing a sub-niche will help you identify your audience?

Our hypothetical blogger has chosen this niche because she practices yoga regularly and has for years. She is passionate about the subject and knows a lot about it. She may not be a yoga instructor, but she is definitely an enthusiast. She will understand the language that yoga practitioners use, and she will already know how to use lingo such as Vinyasa, Namaste, hatha, and such.

Additionally, our yoga enthusiast should make it her goal to tap into the community in the blogosphere that shares her interests. We will learn more about the blogosphere community in chapter 8. As we will see, an important part of building your blogging business will be driving traffic to your site, and the blogosphere community will play a big role in that.

CHAPTER SUMMARY:

1. In chapter 2, we brainstormed topics and niches on which to base your blog.
2. We covered the benefits of niche blogs.

3. Then we walked through the steps that you should take to choose the niche that is right for you.

YOUR QUICK START ACTION STEP:

1. Use a blog search engine to find a blog that fits into the niche you have chosen.
2. Based on the content you find there, decide for yourself if this is the sort of thing that aligns with your long-term goals as a blogger.
3. If not, explore some of the other niches from your list even if you have crossed it off.

Chapter 3: Blogging Business Models

Chapter 3: Blogging Business Models

As stated in Chapter 1, making money with blogs is different from e-commerce websites. Blogs don't sell products directly. The business models discussed in this book fall under what is called performance-based advertising. You, the blogger, partner with merchants and help them sell their products by promoting them on your blog. Say, for example, you have chosen cross-training as your niche. You may want to partner with merchants such as Zappos, Under Armour, or Gatorade. On your blog, you will place advertisements for shoes from Zappos, sports clothing from Under Armour, and sports drinks from Gatorade. The more traffic that flows through your site (meaning, the more visitors who come to your blog to read your posts), the more potential you have to generate revenue for and from your merchants.

There are three distinct types of performance-based advertising: cost-per-click (CPC), cost-per-mile (CPM), and cost-per-acquisition (CPA). Each of these business models works differently and entail different relationships between you and the merchant.

Cost-per-click (CPC)

The cost-per-click advertising generates revenue when a visitor to a website clicks on an ad. The visitor is then redirected to a new website. Therefore, this model of advertising relies on getting the website visitor to take a direct action (clicking on the ad). CPC is useful for businesses who want to bring more traffic to their site.

Several Internet companies specialize in CPC advertising, including Google AdSense, Yahoo Search Marketing, Microsoft Bing Ads, and One by AOL. CPC is a valuable service for businesses. Since the user has to make an intentional decision to click on the ad, the business can measure the effectiveness of their ads.

Cost-per-click ads can be found all over the Web. For instance, Youtube, Reddit, and eBay all use Google AdSense. The blog Mashable (www.mashable.com) generates over $200,000 monthly from CPC advertising via Google Adsense. On the Mashable landing page, for instance, ads are seamlessly displayed alongside blog content. A think menu at the top of the page is upstaged by a large, flashy banner ad 250px tall. CPC advertising made Mashable founder Pete Cashmore a multimillionaire.

Cost-per-mille (CPM)

Also called Cost-per-thousand or cost-per-impression, these types of ads are basic display ads. Revenue is generated based on the number of "impressions" or views. Basically, each time a page with a display ad is clicked, revenue is generated simply by the fact that the visitor has seen the ad.

CPM is ubiquitous across the web. Some of the most successful blogs utilizing CMP include Tuts+ (www.tutsplus.com) and Literally Unbelievable (www.literallyunbelievable.org). Check out these sites, and you will notice how the placement and orientation of the ads complement the site content. CPM ads work best when aligned front and center, or else in the top right sidebar. On the blog, Literally Unbelievable, for instance, blog content is framed on the left, right, and foot by banner ads.

Affiliate marketing: Cost-per-acquisition (CPA)

A third type of online advertising business model is based on the concept of acquisition. Unlike cost-per-click or cost-per-mille, cost-per-acquisition (CPA) entails that the blogger initializes a relationship with external vendors or merchants. The affiliate (you, the blogger) will work as a publisher to spread the word and promote the goods or services of a merchant.

When a visitor comes to your blog, and

he or she clicks on a CPA ad, they will be redirected to the merchant's website. If the visitor then makes a purchase, you (the affiliate) receive a commission from that sale. Stated another way, in the CPA model, your blog functions as a funnel to drive customers to your merchant. Your grateful merchant then gives you a percentage of their profits in return.

Average commission rates vary from 5-30%, and there are a lot of variables as to how the rate is determined such as the type of industry for which you are advertising and the cost of the product. For instance, a CPA ad for a private jet will have a low commission rate whereas an ad for holistic vitamin supplements will tend to be higher. Here's how the math breaks down: the cost of product times percentage equals commission.

We will get more into the specifics of Affiliate marketing in chapter 7.

Benefits of Cost-per Models

Before you put all the effort and energy into developing your blog, it is important to understand how these advertising business models work in the long term. As mentioned in chapter 1, you probably won't become a millionaire overnight. Cashmore developed his Mashable empire over the course of a decade. Once you embrace the business attitude of blogging for profit, you will begin to see its many benefits.

- If you have chosen a niche that you are truly passionate about, writing your blog will be effortless

- Passive income (your blog generates income even when you're not around)
- Work from home
- No-risk investment (it doesn't cost anything to start a blog)
- Access to a global audience

CHAPTER SUMMARY:

In chapter 3, we covered the three business models for advertising on your blog. Cost-per-click, cost-per-mille, and cost-per-acquisition each have their strengths and weaknesses. The good thing is that niche blogging can be effortless; the bad news is that it can take years to build an audience.

YOUR QUICK START ACTION STEP:

1. Get a better grasp of the look and feel of cost-per-click business models by visiting a site that uses Google Adsense. Some of the sites listed in this chapter include Youtube (www.youtube.com), Reddit (www.reddit.com), eBay (ebay.com), and Mashable (www.mashable.com).

2. Take notes.

3. Ask yourself: do the ads fit with the rest of the content on the blog (do the ads look like ads)?

4. Do the products or services being advertised align with the blog's niche audience?

5. Are you tempted to click on the ads, or are they an unpleasant presence?

6. What is your impression of the placement of the ads? Are the ads

placed strategically to attract your attention?

7. What are the sizes of the ads? Is it proportional to the other content on the page?

Chapter 4: Setting Up Your Blog

dedicated ftp statistics
servers
php files support
colocation files php website internet
sftp internet files domain colocation
reliable internet css
storage WEB dedicated
servers
colocation sftp website ftp
reliable mysql
HOSTING
reliable http dedicated
database hosting
dedicated files statistics database
ftp internet colocation
website html website dedicated html
transfer www asp
hosting dedicated support sftp php
ftp
asp

Chapter 4: Setting Up Your Blog

Now it's time to get into the technical nitty-gritty. In just a few steps, you can have your blog set up in under an hour. There are two necessary components that you will need to get started: a custom domain name and a Wordpress.com user account.

There are dozens of blogging platforms out there, some paid and some free. Some free alternatives to Wordpress.com include Blogger and Tumblr. Paid blogging platforms include Weebly, Wix, and Squarespace.

A third option is to lease a private server and install blogging software on it. This option can get pretty advanced, but it will allow you a great deal more flexibility in the look and accessibility of your blog. This option would entail a web hosting account (leased server) via a company such as GoDaddy (www.godaddy.com) and familiarity with the WordPress software (www.wordpress.org).

*Note: Wordpress.org offers open source software for building robust blogs. Wordpress.com is a website that provides free hosting for your blog with a simplified version of the WordPress software, nothing to install.

Domain Names

While the custom domain name is optional, it is an important part of setting up your blog because it will function as your unique identity. Without a custom domain name, the site you create on Wordpress.com will receive an automatic URL: http://www.yourblog.wordpress.com. Not only is this long string of letters and punctuation unsightly; it is hard to remember and generic.

You want your custom domain name to pop! Your domain name should be simple, easy to remember, and directly related to your niche. Say for example you have chosen yoga as your niche. You want to attract an audience interested in leading a holistic, spiritual, active, and mindful lifestyle. A good domain name would be some variation on these keywords. Let's say you decide to name your site Yoga 4 Life. Your domain name would then become: www.yoga4life.com.

Choosing your domain name is like designing a vanity license plate. It's semi-permanent, but you can change it at any time. You can even purchase multiple domains and set them up to direct the same blog.

As you brainstorm potential domain names, begin to collect keywords. If you are coming up short, you can use an online keyword generator like Wordstream (www.wordstream.com). Keyword generators can be an important asset because they take into consideration the popularity of words entered into search engines like Google, Yahoo, and Bing.

*Note: Your list of keywords will also be important when we get to chapter 8, How to Promote Your Blog.

- Your domain name is your unique online identifier.

- It makes your site easy to find because it is a short, simple, and memorable phrase.
- The custom domain name makes it easier for search engines to find you.
- The custom domain name makes it easier for your audience to find you.

Wordpress.com

WordPress is arguably the best and certainly the most popular platform for blogging. It is relatively easy to learn and to use. WordPress provides you with readymade templates (called themes), into which you can plug your unique content. WordPress also supports many ways to customize your blog with custom headers, colors, layouts, and add-ons (called plugins).

Themes are highly flexible while also providing a strong backbone. All themes come with a standard color scheme and layout. You will design your own structure using menus, pages (for static content), and categories into which you will organize your posts.

WordPress also supports a host of interactive features that you can use to reach out to your community. These include RSS feeds, social media integration, followers, comments, likes, and plenty of ways to share your content across the Web.

- Large community of users
- Large library of support materials and help guides

- Libraries of free themes and plugins
- Built-in analytics
- It's free
- It's in the cloud, so you are not tied down to any particular computer or server.
- It's easy to use. No HTML, CSS, or coding are required.

Are you ready to get started? The next section of this chapter provides a step-by-step walkthrough that will take you through the process of choosing and purchasing your domain name, creating a new site, and beginning to customize your theme.

How to Set up Your Blog

1. Hop on over to Wordpress.com
2. Create a new account, if you do not already have one.
3. Log in to WordPress.
4. Click on the button marked "Add New Site."
5. WordPress will work in the background and create your new site.
6. Name your site. The name of your site should be some variation on your domain name. For example, I will title my yoga site "Yoga For Life."
7. Now that you have created your site, browse through the library of themes. Choose a theme that matches the look and feel of your niche.
8. Click on the link to customize your theme. Now it is time to

create a structure for your site. You will need to add a menu and decide how you want your posts to display.

9. If you are blogging about multiple topics, create categories. For example, on my "Yoga for Life" site, I will create two categories: one for my favorite yoga poses and a second for mindful meditation practices.

10. Add your categories to your menu.

11. You also have the option of creating static pages. Pages can host information such as a mission statement, contact, or bio.

12. Add any pages you have created to your menu.

13. As you continue to customize your blog, you can consider adding widgets, photos, custom colors, and more. For now, we have gone through all the steps to get your new blog up and running.

14. As soon as your site goes live, WordPress will lead you through the process of customizing your site with a unique icon, tagline, photos, and more. You will find information on how to do that on your dashboard.

Register your Custom Domain Name

15. First, we're going to choose your domain name.

16. Remember your keywords list? Choose a simple, memorable phrase.

17. In Wordpress.com, you will need to sign up for a plan to receive a custom domain name. Otherwise, in the example of "Yoga For Life," without a custom domain, the URL will be: www.yogaforlife.wordpress.com.

18. In your dashboard in WordPress, click on the link for "Plan." WordPress offers three types of plans which vary in cost from $4-$25 per month.

19. Choose a plan, and click "Upgrade."

20. Click through the next few steps to upgrade your plan.

21. Back on your dashboard next to "Domain," click "Add."

22. In the search bar, type in the first choice for your domain name.

23. It is likely that your preferred domain name has already been taken. If so, WordPress will generate some variations. For instance, if www.yoga4life.com is already owned by someone else, I have the option of choosing www.yoga4life.blog or moving down my list of preferred domain names.

24. Once you have settled on a domain, click "Select."

25. You're all set!

CHAPTER SUMMARY:

In this chapter, we learned the ABC's of WordPress. We covered a lot of new concepts and vocabulary, including web hosting, theme, and plugin. You followed the steps to create your new blog and registered your domain name. In the next chapter, you will write your first post!

YOUR QUICK START ACTION STEP:

1. As a new WordPress user, you will benefit from learning the ins and outs of the platform. Head on over to support.wordpress.com to learn everything you need to know to get started.

2. Start by browsing the "Getting Started" area.

3. Get a handle on the lingo. You may encounter unfamiliar words.

4. Even if you are not yet ready to fully customize your site, you can save time in the future by

exploring themes, customizable options, plug-ins, and widgets.

Chapter 5: Writing Your First Blog Post

BLOGGING

Chapter 5: Writing Your First Blog Post

Now that you're a WordPress user, you can start blogging! In this chapter, we will walk through the process of writing and publishing your first blog post.

First of all, let's clarify the difference between a page and a post. The fundamental difference between a website and a blog is that websites are composed of static pages, full of information that does not change on a regular basis. Blogs, on the other hand, are primarily composed of posts. If you are familiar with the way social media platforms work, WordPress posts can be compared to a Facebook or a Twitter stream. If you're a pen and paper type of person, posts can be compared to the daily entries you write in your journal every day. Posts appear on your blog in reverse chronological order (newer to older). Visitors to your blog will see your most recent posts first at the top of your homepage. That way, your blog will appear as if it were current, that is, as long as you post regularly, frequently, and consistently.

WordPress has become the favorite choice for bloggers worldwide because of its ease of use and large user base. Compared to the other options out there, like Blogger and Tumblr, WordPress is the go-to platform for both novice and experienced bloggers for a variety of reasons.

So, let's get started. Here are the steps you will follow each time you go about writing and publishing a new post.

1. In your sidebar, there are buttons for publishing new content: pages, posts, and media. Click on the "Add" button next to "Blog Post."

2. At the top of the page, there is a space to add a title to your post. Begin by adding your title. The title of my first post on Yoga4Life will be: "Welcome Yoga enthusiasts!"

3. Your first post will state the purpose or mission of your blog. You will want to welcome visitors to your new site.

4. Over time, as more and more posts accumulate in your blog, the welcome post will appear at the very end of your list of posts. That is to say, your blog posts are automatically arranged in reverse

chronological order. The reasoning behind this is that the newest information and updates are intended to be the first thing that visitors to your site will see.

5. After composing the text for your first post and formatting it to make it look visually appealing, proofread your text for spelling and grammar.

6. Like any word processing program, controls for formatting your text appear in a control bar located between the post title and the body text.

7. If you break up your body text into short paragraphs, it will make your blog more readable and much more visually appealing.

8. You can also toggle between a visual display and the HTML (code) display. For most intents and purposes, you can ignore the HTML tab.

9. Then, to make your first post visually appealing, move your attention to the right sidebar on your screen. This is called the "Post Settings" sidebar. There are five tabs: Status, Categories & Tags, Features Image, Sharing, and More Options.

10. The Status tab displays information about the time and date that your post has been published. This is also the place where you will publish or schedule your post to be published. We will cover more on this topic in the next chapter.

11. The Categories and Tags tab allows you to organize your post into a category.

12. Adding photos to your post in-line with text will help to integrate the ads on your page with the rest of your content. You don't want your ads to be either distracting or overwhelming in comparison to the rest of the content on your site. We will discuss more about the placement of ads in chapter 7.

"Welcome Yoga enthusiasts!"
Yoga For Life has officially launched! We here at Yoga For Life are looking forward to the opportunity to provide you with quality content related to the practice

and spirituality of yoga. We welcome yoga practitioners of all levels and styles. Stick with us on and off the mat. Our site is 100% mobile friendly.
Bookmark our site and make sure to come back regularly for the best new yoga poses, daily inspiration, and mindful meditation practices!

Subscribe to our newsletter to stay up to date with us. We hope you are as excited as we are, and that you will join us on our journey toward practicing a more mindful and holistic life.

TIP: Remember, your blog posts will never go away (unless you delete them). It's important to understand that your first blog post will be published and visible to the public, and will continue to be as long as your WordPress account remains active. If, at some point in the future, you decide to alter your sub-niche or change your niche altogether, make sure to explore your archived posts to check for relevance. Consistency matters.

CHAPTER SUMMARY:

In this chapter, we learned about the technical requirements of what you need to know about posting content on your blog. We discussed the layout and features of the blog post management area. We also discussed tips related to visual formatting and the design of posts.

YOUR QUICK START ACTION STEP:

This chapter covered the step-by-step process that you will need to become familiar with as a new blogger. It can be a lot to take in; we're covering a lot of information in a short amount of space in this guide. Here's one way that you can make your life easier as you get the hang of it.

1. Schedule a time to sit down and learn the WordPress platform.

2. Take it in strides. Begin by gaining a grasp of the dashboard (your home base).

3. Browse articles on the support.wordpress.com to brush up on particular topics.

4. Particularly when it comes to customizing your blog, there are myriad options. There are so many options, in fact, that you

probably won't immediately be aware of just how flexible WordPress is.

5. Begin by going through the instructions above for composing, formatting, and publishing posts.

6. Then, explore your options for structuring your blog using categories. While using categories is not a requirement, they can make it far easier to control the layout of your site. Remember, your goal is to attract visitors especially repeat visitors. One easy way to do this is by structuring your blog in a way that is easily navigable.

Chapter 6: Managing and Scheduling Your Blog Posts

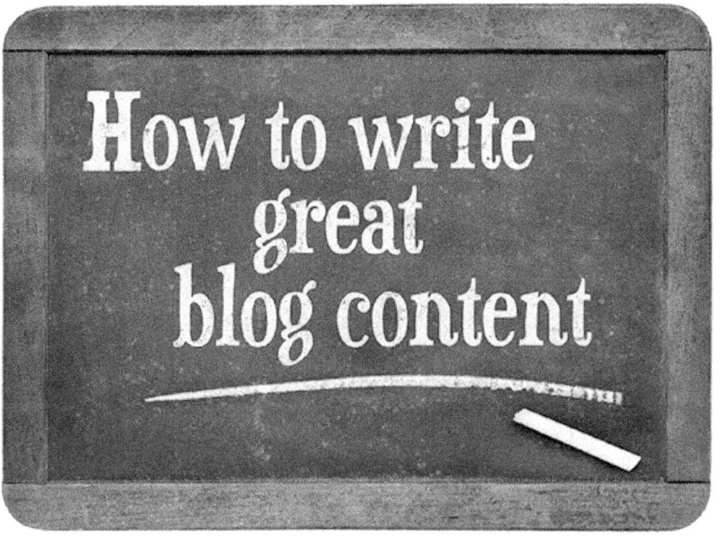
How to write
great
blog content

Chapter 6: Managing and Scheduling Your Blog Posts

Now that you have written your first blog post, it's time to put some thought into how to structure your blog, organize your posts, and manage your schedule. Visitors who frequent blogs expect new content. Stated another way, bloggers who post regularly and frequently give off the impression that they are reliable, fervent about their niche, and loyal to their audience. Your successful blog will thrive only as long as you keep your content current, dynamic, and versatile.

In this chapter, we will cover three things you will need to know. We will go over how to structure your blog to make it easily navigable through the use of categories. We will walk through the process of managing categories and adding them to your menu. Finally, we will cover the technical process of scheduling blog posts.

After covering these simple steps, you will then have a site that is intuitively structured. You will also come away with a consistent plan for publishing content that will save you a great deal of time and unnecessary complications in the days and months to come.

Categories

Why should you use categories?

Think of categories as folders in a filing cabinet. We want to be organized so that we don't lose track of our paperwork (i.e., posts). A good strategy is to organize your papers into folders so that when you come back later looking for a particular document, you will be able to find it easily based on what folder it belongs in. For instance, my filing cabinet includes folders for bills, medical, school, keepsakes, and correspondence. If my filing cabinet were a blog, each of these folders would be analogous to a category. Every time I pay a bill, I place the statement in my bills folder. Correspondingly, every time you write a post about school, you will place it in the school category.

How should you use categories?

"Yoga For Life" is structured simply with two categories: "Yoga Postures" and "Mindful Meditation." My first post "Welcome Yoga enthusiasts" don't relate to either of these categories so we're going to leave it as uncategorized. In my next post, however, I am going to break down my favorite Vinyasa. Using a combination of text and images so that beginning practitioners can more easily follow along, I will lead my visitors through mountain, forward fold, downward dog, chaturanga, baby cobra, and then back to mountain. I will call this post "My Go-To Vinyasa," and I will categorize it in the "Yoga Postures."

So you see, WordPress categories are just like filing folders. They make it easy for you and your visitors to find the information they're looking for. The additional benefit of categories is that it makes your site far easier to navigate. In the following steps, we will walk through how to break out your niche into sub-niches. These sub-niches will become your categories.

1. First, you will need to know what topics you will be blogging about. Return to your niche. What topics might your audience be interested in reading about that relate directly to your niche?

2. While brainstorming a topic, ensure that your categories are distinct, and they do not overlap too much.

3. As stated above, Yoga4Life.com has two categories: "Yoga Postures" and "Mindful Meditation." To generate a loyal reader base, I want my site to be easy to navigate. I will place my two topics on the menu at the top of the page under my heading banner.

4. Go back to the post you published in the last chapter. In the right-

hand sidebar, open the tab for Categories & Tabs.

5. Click "Add New Category."

6. Name your category.

7. For each new post, you will return to this area in the right-hand sidebar to associate it with a category. Posts associated with a category will only appear in that category in a list arranged in reverse chronological order. You can also utilize the option of "Uncategorized" for posts that are not associated with any of your topics.

8. Now we will add your categories to the menu so that your visitors will be able to read your categorized posts. From your dashboard in WordPress, go to Themes and click the

"Customize" button. This is where you will create both the categories as well as the menus into which you will place them.

9. Click on the tab marked "Menus." The location and number of menus on your site depend on which theme you are using. Click on either your primary menu (if available), or create a new menu.

10. Click "Add Items."

11. Open the tab marked "Categories.

12. Click on the plus signs next to the categories you want to add to your menu.

13. Voila! Your categories are now visible and searchable on your menu and ready for your visitors to browse.

14. Always remember to save your work.

Scheduling Posts

Save time by scheduling your posts. WordPress posts can be set to automatically publish on a certain day and at a certain time. It's not precisely automation, but it's just as effective. That's one of the great things about WordPress. Not only is it pretty easy to use, but it's also loaded with robust features to make your business thrive while taking the extra work out of your inbox.

Take this scenario, for instance. You have a long block of free time on Sunday, and you want to put some time into beefing up your blog. You've been underwhelmed by the traffic your blog has been generating. Here's a simple thing you can do to effectively and productively increase traffic to your blog in a single block of time.

It's a common misconception that maintaining a blog requires a large amount of time spread across just about every day of the week. But you don't have to check your blog every day to keep it updated. Using the strategy of scheduling posts will give off the impression to your audience that you are present as well as productive.

Let's take a look at how to schedule your posts for future publication dates and/or times.

1. Remember in the last chapter when we walked through the "Post Settings" sidebar? Let's return to your first blog post and

take another look at how to control the ways your posts are published.

2. Under "Post Settings," expand the "Status" tab.

3. You will see a drop-down menu entitled "Publish Immediately."

4. When you click the drop-down button, a calendar will open up.

5. To schedule a series of posts for future publication, first compose and proof your drafts.

6. Before you close or navigate away from your post, click the "Status" tab.

7. Open the menu and select the date on which you would like the post to become public.

8. You can also set the time of day that the post will publish on that future date.

9. By default, the post automatically sets to publish at the time of your present writing.

10. Some tips for scheduling posts include setting your posts to publish at a regular time every day or week. Selecting a time of day during regular working hours is optimal. That is, if your visitors notice that you are publishing posts at odd times during the night, they might suspect that your blog is automated. This can turn readers off. Your goal should be to appear authentic.

Set Your Time Zone

Unless you are writing for a target audience on the other side of the planet, you will want to ensure that your blog is publishing posts in the time and date of your current time zone. This might sound like a trivial matter. However, if a visitor navigates to your site and notices that your most recent post was published at 3 o'clock in the morning Japan time, they might become suspicious.

11. As a final measure, remember to set your time zone in your site's settings.

12. In your dashboard, click on "Settings." It's the last item in the left-hand sidebar.

13. This area includes dozens of settings that will not only help you promote your blog (more on this in chapter 8) but also edit information that you plugged in to the site as you were creating it.

14. At the bottom of the "Site Profile" area, you will find the setting for "site time zone. It is automatically set for UTC+0 (Greenwich Mean Time aka London, UK). You can easily change this to orient your blog to your local time zone by typing in a major city close to your home location.

15. To customize yoga4life.com to my local time zone, I typed in New York, NY so that my readers will know that I am located on the Eastern seaboard of the U.S.

CHAPTER SUMMARY:

In this chapter, we covered two easy strategies you can use to manage and schedule your blog. First, we covered the importance and technical aspects related to how categories are used to structure your blog. Then we walked through the process of scheduling posts which will save you a great deal of time in the long run.

YOUR QUICK START ACTION STEP:

If you thought that using categories and scheduling posts would make your life easier, here's an additional strategy you can use to make it infinitely more streamlined.

As we will learn in chapter 10, WordPress pairs well with other cloud platforms out there. Like a good wine and cheese combo, WordPress and Google pair well together, and using them in collaboration can make your life a whole lot easier. In the following steps, we will walk through a process that you can use to link Google Calendar with WordPress to help you keep track of the schedule of your posts.

Some benefits include ensuring the regularity and timing of your content. Your audience will be much happier and eager to consistently return to your site on a regular basis if you can commit to publishing posts according to a consistent and regular schedule.

You can use Google Calendar or any other calendar software (Apple iCal or Microsoft Outlook) to track your posts. Planning out your posts by day, week and month greatly ease the effort required to keep up the regularity of a commercial blog. Using a calendar software will also help make your blog as efficient as possible.

1. Begin by brainstorming on the topics you want to write on over any given amount of time. For instance, over the course of a month, you may want to post about a variety of topics. On Yoga4Life, I will be posting about poses every other week and adding daily inspirations for mindful meditation.

2. Instead of logging in every day to add the meditations, I will take a few hours on one calm Sunday to compose my posts for the month. I will paste my text into individual posts, and then schedule those posts to automatically publish daily over the course of the month.

3. You could take it an extra step further by choosing themes on

which to write about and switching up your themes each month.

4. In Google Calendar, create a new calendar with the same title as your blog.

5. Decide which day or days of the week you want to publish new posts. You can also label your posts in the calendar app by adding custom colors associated with a given category.

6. You can either add individual events for unique posts or else create a repeating event to remind you of upcoming posts per theme or category.

As indicated in the month-by-month schedule laid out in the steps above, blogging is a long-term activity. Keeping a close eye on your schedule by using a calendar will help you stay organized. But there's more to it than that. In chapter 9, we will take a closer look at what it takes for you, the blogger, to succeed in the long run, not just month by month, but year by year.

If you recall the case of Pete Cashmore of Mashable, as discussed in chapter 3, he had the ambition as well as the patience to stick to the blogging game for a decade. That stick-to-itiveness made him a multi-millionaire. Before you move on to the next chapter, you should decide for yourself if you have that kind of stick-to-itiveness to keep up with the lifestyle of a blogger.

Chapter 7: How Blogging Makes You Money

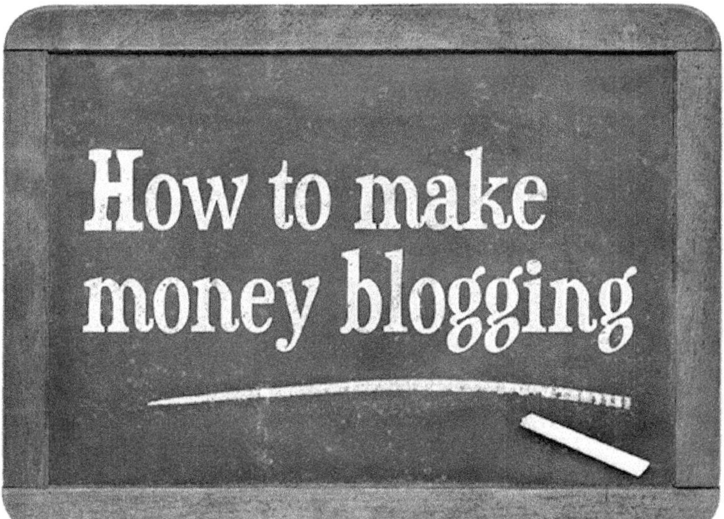
How to make
money blogging

Chapter 7: How Blogging Makes You Money

In this chapter, we will get into the nitty-gritty of how to profit from the advertising on your blog. We will be focusing on the third business model discussed in chapter 3, cost-per-acquisition (CPA), also known as Affiliate marketing. As discussed in chapter 3, the Affiliate marketing business model is built on the relationship between the affiliate (you the blogger) and a merchant (the sponsor of the advertising and the maker of the goods or service). Let's take a closer look at what this relationship entails, and how it works.

There are actually four parties involved in making Affiliate marketing work, the affiliate, the merchant, the affiliate network, and the consumer.

Role of the Affiliate

As the affiliate, you play the role of content publisher. Your blog hosts content related to the products that you advertise on your site. Visitors who come to your site are looking first for the information discussed in your blog, and secondly for the products that you are promoting via the ads embedded all across your site. Your role is to draw an audience to your site through attractive and intriguing information in the form of blog posts.

Your posts can be thematic, taking the form of categories based on sub-niches. Alternatively, they could utilize the form of storytelling. Another way to go about it would be to post stand-alone reviews or commentary based on your particular niche. That being said, every page and post on your site would display ads that link to products associated with your niche.

Role of the Affiliate Network

Let's take a look at the role of the affiliate network in moderating sales, ads, and commissions. Affiliate networks are 3rd party sites that connect publishers (you the affiliate) with merchants. The most popular affiliate networks are:

- ClickBank.com
- CJ Affiliate by Conversant (CJ.com)
- Linkshare.com
- Performics.com

- ShareaSale.com

While it is possible to form relationships directly with sponsors and merchants, affiliate networks make the work of CPA infinitely less complicated. They provide a valuable service by connecting publishers (you the affiliate) with merchants. The networks listed above host catalogs on their websites.

Role of the Merchant

Let's consider the relationship between the affiliate (you) and the merchant. Since the affiliate network mediates the relationship between the affiliate and the merchant, that means that you will only ever have an indirect relationship with your sponsor. You should remember, however, that the relationship is entirely mutually beneficial. Affiliate marketing is based on what is known as revenue sharing. That means that, at the same time that you are providing a service for the merchant by promoting their product or products, the merchant also benefits from the services that you are providing for them. You get to choose which products to promote, and the more traffic you are able to direct to their site, the more revenue will be generated. The affiliate and the merchant share in the revenue.

Role of the Consumer

You, as the affiliate, take on the responsibility of promoting the merchant's product. Through a combination of targeted blog posts and strategically placed ads, you direct traffic to your merchant's e-commerce site. "Traffic," in this case also refers to visitors, also known as the browsers on the web or consumers.

Back in chapter 1, we discussed the importance of switching your mindset from casual or personal blogging to a business model. When considering the role of the consumer, you might start to think of the visitors to your site less as information-seekers and more as consumers. Generating site traffic is one of your primary goals. Consumers are your audience, and the only demographic capable of driving revenue to your merchant sponsors.

Commission Rates

While it is thrilling to believe that your blog can generate thousands of dollars of revenue for you like magic, in reality, you have little control over the choices that consumers actually make. Myriad factors affect the choices that consumers make. It is not the goal of this book to offer insight into either consumer psychology or market forces.

However, we do have control over the choices that we make in several important areas:

- Choice of the niche market
- Choice of the industry
- Choice of the products to promote
- Composition of post content
- Placement of ads

There is no magic key to answering these questions for you. In some cases, it may come down to trial and error, but ideally, you will find success through the thoughtful and strategic planning through the use of your business acumen.

In short, your niche blog should automatically be associated with some industry or another. Let's refer back to the list of categories and niches in chapter 2. For instance, your Paleo cooking blog will host ads located in the Food, Wine and Cooking category under which you can find sub-categories for products including cookbooks, dieting products, and specialty kitchen supplies.

You may have noticed that Clickbank, like other affiliate networks, categorize their products according to industry. It is important to realize that some niche markets are more lucrative than others when it comes to Affiliate marketing. According to a recent study, Affiliate marketing in the industries of electronics, books, and media are among the less profitable. On the other end of the spectrum, Affiliate marketing of health products and finance software and services have recently been on the rise.

That being said, your blog will succeed to a greater extent if you follow the advice laid out in chapter 1. Choose a niche that you are passionate about because it will give you the impetus to keep at it in the long run.

First, a caveat. Learning how to profit from Affiliate marketing can be tricky even for those who have been at it for years. There are a lot of variables, the main one being commission rates.

If Affiliate marketing still seems

mystifying to you, head on over to clickbank.com/university. There, you will find motivational and informative tutorials and videos that will help you get started.

Chapter 3 discussed Affiliate marketing in brief. In this chapter, we will be taking a closer look at Affiliate marketing (also known as cost-per-acquisition, or CPA), and go through the steps of how to set up your blog with CPA ads.

In this chapter, we will work together to create a strategic plan for promoting pet-related items for a website called DoggieLove101.blog. This blog will feature a robust structure that includes categories for walking and training, agility, grooming, pet care, pet health, food, and reviews of pet care supplies.

Now, let's hop over to an affiliate network, and take a look at what categories they have to offer in terms of products available for you to promote on your niche blog.

*Note: Before you can start using ClickBank, you will need to create an account. This entails entering your Tax ID or SSN and acknowledging a client contract.

1. Go to ClickBank.com.
2. Find the area on their website that hosts their catalog of product ads.
3. For the purposes of our exercise, we will navigate to the Animal Care and Pets section which is nestled under the Home and Garden category.

4. At the moment, one of ClickBank's featured products is the *German Shepherd Handbook*. Seeing as how you are so passionate about your niche category, you will already know some things about German Shepherds, their behavior, their demeanor, their appearance, etc.

5. You will want to compose a new post on your blog related to German Shepherds based on an aspect of the dog breed that you are already familiar with. To save you time, go with your gut. This may seem counterintuitive, but your goal here is less to inform your readers about the demeanor of German Shepherds as it is to direct their attention to the ad

that you have placed within the post.

6. Remember, we're operating according to a business mindset. Our goal is to promote products and push traffic to merchants. The content of your blog post matters less than the relationship between your niche market and the product that you are promoting.

7. Once you identify a product that you are interested in promoting, locate its hoplink. A HopLink is an URL that you will copy and paste into your blog.

*Note: More information about the technical aspects of linking ads via HopLinks can be found in your Affiliate Network's support site.

Promoting Your Merchant's Product on Your Blog

Now, we will return to your blog, and create the ad.

The HopLink isn't your average URL. When pasted into a web browser, an URL directs you to a particular web page. A HopLink does that too while also keeping track of how much traffic and how much sales are being generated between your blog and your merchant!

Here is where your creative instinct comes into play. Refer back to the example we looked at back in chapter 3, Mashable.com. Notice how ads, blog content and, and other media are formatted seamlessly in a grid format on this blog's landing page? This should be your goal.

Here are some simple steps designed to help you figure out how and where to place the HopLink in your post.

1. First, you will compose your post and choose which product with which it will be associated. In this example, we will use the German Shepherd book.

2. Experts advise that blog visitors react best to ads placed in the sidebars. That being said, banner ads at the header or footer of pages can be highly attractive clickbait! You can also place HopLinks in the body of your post in line with the text.

3. Each of these options can be instrumented in different ways.

4. To place an ad at the top or bottom of the page, insert the

HopLink in the body of the text. You can do this by clicking the button in the edit bar that looks like a paper clip.

5. To place the ad in the sidebar, create a widget.

Widgets

Widgets are one of the more technical properties of WordPress, but they are also one of its more flexible and practical features. That being said, different themes support widgets in different ways. Let's take for example the 2016 WordPress theme ("Twenty Sixteen"). This theme launches automatically with a single- centered column and places widgets in a right-hand sidebar.

1. From the WordPress dashboard, click on "Customize" adjacent to "Themes" in the left-hand sidebar.
2. Click on the "Widgets" tab in the left-hand sidebar.
3. Click "Add a widget."
4. Here you have two options. Scroll all the way to the bottom of the list and select "Text: Arbitrary Text." This widget supports plain text as well as HTML code.
5. Toggle to the "text" panel.
6. Paste your HopLink here.
7. Don't forget to save.

If you experience errors with the site appearance and/or its code, double-check the URL formatting. The HopLink should look like this:

<a href=["hoplink"]>[Text]</a>

*Tip: you can also add images to Widgets using the "Add Media" button.

CHAPTER SUMMARY:

In this chapter, we walked through the details of affiliate advertising (CPA). First, we learned about affiliate networks. Then we stepped through the processes necessary for identifying and inserting HopLinks into our blogs.

*Note: Additional information about how to monetize your WordPress site can be found in the support section of WordPress at the following link:

support.wordpress.com/monetize-your-site/

YOUR QUICK START ACTION STEP:

Aligning blog content and product promotion can be a time-consuming process. Now let's choose a time to put these instructions into practice. Head back over to the calendar you created in the last chapter. Add a new event. Find some time to chisel out of your schedule to go through the steps laid out in this chapter.

1. Browse the sites of the affiliate networks listed in this chapter
2. Sign up for one or more affiliate networks.

3. Choose a handful of products you are interested in promoting.
4. Consider some strategies that you could use to promote these products via blog posts.

Chapter 8: How to Promote Your Blog

PROMOTION

Chapter 8: How to Promote your Blog

The key to generating income from a monetized blog is in driving web traffic to your site. There are plenty of tools available to achieve this goal. Some are technical, and some are social. Depending on your natural proclivities and intended audience, you can use the strategies discussed in this chapter and in chapter 10 to increase traffic coming in and out of your site!

When you're online, it's not exactly like you can get out a loudspeaker to rally your troops. So how do bloggers do it? Promoting your blog, like any other website, includes a plethora of tools engineered to maximize traffic to your site. These tools work in a variety of ways.

Ever wonder how search engines work? How does Google translate your search query into a list of results? It's all based on the keywords that web designers and bloggers put on their sites.

Here's Google's explanation as to how its algorithms work. In essence, "Google ranking systems sort through the hundreds of billions of web pages in our Search index to give you useful and relevant results in a fraction of a second." So, how can you use this system to your advantage? Reminder, no coding knowledge necessary.

What Is SEO?

The most common and well-known toolkit for promoting blogs and websites is called "search engine optimization" (SEO). The goal of SEO is to hack the search engine's algorithm to bid for a better ranking. Like affiliate networks, search engines connect blogs and other websites to those who are searching the web; call them site visitors, consumers, web traffic, what have you.

WordPress comes pre-loaded with a plethora of tools for optimizing your search engine ranking. You can read more about these features on support.wordpress.com. WordPress's business plan makes it easy to find and install SEO plugins, the most popular of which is called Yoast (yoast.com). That would be the easy way.

Hacking with Keywords

With the free personal plan, there are still plenty of options. In WordPress, your metadata is located all across your site in the form of post titles. One strategy would be to use your list of keywords creatively.

Remember back in chapter 4 when we came up with a list of keywords? A simple way to drive traffic to your site will be to add keywords. This is where that list comes back into play.

Scatter your meaty keywords across your site title, post titles, page titles, subtitles, etc. Doing so will help search engines figure out what your site is about. It will make it easier for search engines like Google and Bing to match you with those who are searching for the information you have to offer.

Other tools and strategies for promoting your blog and generating a following include integrating social media (we'll cover this in chapter 10), publishing a newsletter, and becoming an active member in your niche community in the blogosphere.

Getting Google's Attention

You may be wondering how Google decides what order in which to display search results? First of all, the pages within a search query are known by the acronym SERP which stands for search engine results page.

If you're interested in learning more about the ranking of your blog or someone else's, go check out www.SERPwatcher.com. This site offers robust tools to help you identify your location on a SERP, increase your ranking, and track your progress.

Basically, when a person opens up Google, they will use any number of common strategies to pull up the kind of information they are looking for. For instance, if the browser is looking for tips on how to improve their mindful meditation practice, they might enter:

- "tips on how to improve my mindful meditation practice"
- "how to practice mindful meditation"
- "meditation techniques"
- "how to be more patient and mindful"
- "what can I do to be more patient and mindful during meditation?"

You'll notice that all these phrases have some common keywords. In order to connect with your target audience, you will want to fill your site with words that browsers will be looking for.

On the resulting SERP, Google decides which sites to display first based on hundreds of factors. Google uses an algorithm called PageRank to decide which pages to display and in what order. Ironically, the algorithm is named after inventor Larry Page, not because it ranks pages. Some important factors include:

- Domain name and how long it's been active
- Keywords embedded in your site's and page's header
- Location of page on site
- Amount of information on page and size of page (in bytes)

- How often you edit/update your
  site
- Amount of ads in relation to
  content.
- Inbound and outbound links
  (how many sites you link to and
  how many sites link to you.

This last factor is why building your
social network in the blogosphere is so
important. The more bloggers who know
about your site and respect your
authority, the more likely it will be that
others will embed links to your site on
theirs.

Additionally, if the number of ads on
any given page outweighs the amount of
content, Google will be less inclined to
display your site. They even have a name
for sites like these. They call them "thin

affiliate sites."

Let's Talk Keywords

In the previous section, we discussed the process through which a browser goes through to find information on the web. You will drive traffic to your site by loading your pages with keywords that your audience is most likely to be searching for. So, how do you figure out which words to choose?

We will go about this in a similar way that we brainstormed for your niche. If you've chosen a niche that is a good fit for you, this part should not be too hard. Start with the big ideas. For instance, on DoggieLove101.blog, include these keywords first in its header: dog, pet, animal, critter, grooming, care, supplies, tips, treatment.

Now break each of these categories into subtopics. My first set of words are all about animals. My second set of words are all about pet care. What will my audience be searching for within these two related topics?

- dandruff
- brush
- shampoo
- clipper
- flea
- tick
- Frontline
- PetSmart

Here are some additional tips on how to go about generating keywords:

- Use a thesaurus.
- Imagine what is going through the mind of a hypothetical user.
- Imagine possible blog post topics
- If you come up blank, use a keyword generator. For instance, adwords.google.com has a powerful keyword planner that can help you come up with a list of metadata.

In HTML (HyperText Markup Language) or the underlying code on which your page is displayed in a web browser), the header looks like this:

```
<html>

<head>
```

```
<meta name="description"
    content="Doggie Love 101: Where
    doggies come to be loved">

 <meta name="keywords" content="dog
    pet animal critter grooming care
    supplies tips treatment">

</head>

<body>

The content of the document......

</body>

</html>
```

Anything above <body> does not display
for the viewer. The purpose of the
header is to allow your site to
communicate with other software

running on the Web (i.e. Google).

Your keywords will be entered in the meta tag along with a description of your site. In technical terms, keywords and descriptions are known as "metadata". That's information about other information or the information about the content of your site. Include as many words as you want in the metadata.

Note: Plugins and SEO tools are only available with WordPress's Business plan. They are not supported in the free version.

The Blogosphere Community

Another strategy that bloggers use to

promote their business is to build relationships with other bloggers within their niche through the use of comment threads. Contributing to conversations in response to blog posts is more of an art than a science. We will learn more about how to enable, disable, and modify comments on your blog in Chapter 10. For the moment, all you need to know is that comments can be turned on and off. If comments are enabled on a blog, any visitor can leave a message in response to a post, and it will appear in threads at the bottom of the page after the post content.

Commenting on other blogs can be a useful strategy for promoting your blog for several reasons. First, you can add links in comments which means that the blogger as well as his or her readers can find your site while reading another person's blog on the same subject. Secondly, commenting on the blogs of others can be a powerful social networking strategy. You should be encouraged to build relationships with other bloggers and their audiences who write and read about your niche and sub-niche in the blogosphere.

When commenting on the blogs of others, you want to grab their attention. But be careful not to be forceful or aggressive. The first time you post on the blog of a stranger, think of it as a first date. Leave a good impression by responding to the content of their post thoughtfully. You may not want to begin promoting your own blog right away. Why not wait until date 5 to propose?

*Note: Sometimes commenting on the blogs of others can go terribly awry. By following a few fundamental rules, you can ensure that your presence in the blogosphere is congenial and positive.

- Don't be a "troll." Trolls are blogosphere commenters who have developed a bad reputation for rudely inserting themselves into conversations. Trolls post obnoxious, incendiary, or otherwise off-topic comments. Whether they know it or not, trolls have a negative presence on the blogs of others. For example, don't post an ad for a product you are promoting with a link to your website without also contributing to the conversation and/or commenting on the post above.

- Similarly, don't post long and rambling comments. Good comments are pithy.
- Don't overload your comment with links. If you are going to include a link, make it relevant to the post and tack it on at the end. You will want to avoid giving off the impression that you are only hanging around to sell something.
- Good posts are meaningful. Don't ignore the content of the post and the conversation to which you are contributing.

Tip: Once you have developed strong relationships with others within your niche in the blogosphere, consider soliciting guest writers. People don't just read blogs to find information. One of the strongest aspects of the blogosphere and what makes it a unique galaxy on the Web is its ability to bring like-minded people together. If you can develop relationships with other respected bloggers who write about the same topic as you, it's a possibility that they could help you promote your site by writing a guest post that would drive their readers to your site.

CHAPTER SUMMARY:

Besides promoting products via Affiliate marketing, one of the primary purposes of your site will be to attract traffic from across the web. In this chapter, we looked at several ways to do just that. The primary way to direct traffic to your WordPress blog will be in the form of keywords (that is, unless you upgrade to a business plan which supports SEO plugins).

YOUR QUICK START ACTION STEP:

In this chapter, we have taken a quick look at some of the ways a novice blogger may optimize site traffic. But there are miles to go from here. Think of this chapter as a very brief introduction. Now it's your turn to dig further. Here are some steps that you can take to learn more about how to promote your blog.

Let's get started with SEO! In addition to using plugins, commenting on the blogs of others, and adding metadata to your blog, there are tons of other SEO strategies you can benefit from to promote your blog and drive traffic to your site. Google isn't just a search engine. It's got a massive suite of tools for creating media, managing data, and collaborating online. Here are some Google tools you should know about which will help you further promote your blog:

1. Create a Google Account that you will associate with your blog and business.
2. By collecting all of your information under one Google account, especially created to use for your blog business, it will allow you to create a unique identity for your blog distinct from your own presence on the web for either personal or professional purposes.
3. A Google account links up all of these services: Gmail, YouTube,

Google+, Maps, Play, Books, Translate, Drive, Docs, Calendar, Sheets, Slides, and more.

4. Your Google account will also give you access to a service called My Business.

5. Once you have completed the process of creating a Google account, go to business.google.com.

6. Not only can My Business help you manage the promotion of your site, it could become a powerful tool to drive traffic to your site.

7. My Business supports ad listings and Google Maps location-based listings.

8. In the event that your blog is site-specific, having your blog

business show up on Google Maps will be an important asset.

9. By listing your blog business, My Business also links up with AdWords which supports SEO as well as advertising on Google.

Chapter 9: Scaling Up Your Blog Business to $10,000 a Month

Chapter 9: Scaling Up Your Blog Business to $10,000 a Month

From niche selection to promoting the blog, now that everything has been set up, this chapter will provide additional insight into how to think about how to scale up your blogging business.

Starting a blog is no different from launching a start-up. Both endeavors are scary. They're equally hard. Both require a long-term vision to ensure that the business succeeds.

Remember the mindset transition we talked about in chapter 1? Let's flip the script. Let's stop thinking about the content or the topic of your blog, and start thinking about why your audience should be visiting your blog: click for acquisition.

In chapter 1, we also discussed the case of Pete Cashmore of Mashable. Even despite the irony, his surname didn't make him a millionaire. Neither did the idea of launching a popular blog. People like Cashmere succeed because they embrace a long-term vision and have the patience to see it through. Let's consider the benefits of appreciating and acknowledging the long-term vision.

- Turn your readers into consumers.
- Increase your audience.
- Use SEO (covered in chapter 8).
- Integrate social media (covered in chapter 10).

So how do you set up a blog as a business? It's all about maintaining a careful balance between your content and the products you promote. It's incredibly easy to turn off your readers by overloading your site with ads. Stated another way, you need to consider the design and layout of your site (the visual side) and embrace a respect for your audience (the social side).

Once you begin to realize that your blog is no different from a start-up business, you will realize that the technical side of things (basically everything we covered in chapters 4, 5, and 6) is just the work you need to do to get your business off the ground. It may take you years to develop a solid foundation (your audience). All this can be accomplished through an intelligent use of SEO and social media integration.

Let's take a moment to recap the journey we have taken so far. As we look ahead at long-term goals, it is crucial to appreciate the baby steps. Stated another way, the devil is in the details. Building your blog as a business is a long-term project composed of many steps. Thinking strategically about each decision you have made and will make could mean the difference between a successful blog business and a flop.

Building Your Blog Business from Mindset to Execution

So, let's comprehend the big picture:

- We began by switching our mindset from the writerly, amateur blogger to the business person.
- Then we explored niche markets, and why it is important to think carefully about how the topic of your blog relates to other aspects

of your professional and personal life.

- We took a comprehensive tour of the WordPress blogging platform.
- We also decided upon a site title and took strategic steps to purchase an associated custom domain name.
- After learning about three blog business models, we took a broad tour of Affiliate marketing, networks, and techniques for integrating CPA advertising into your blog.
- Then we took a brief but important stopover in the land of SEO. We learned a few simple ways to identify your target audience and how to reach out to them.

So, in the next chapter, we will look at

how to beef up your blog with social media. We will also tackle some strategies you can use to integrate rich media. Together, these strategies will take your blog business to the next level in style and performance.

CHAPTER SUMMARY:

Launching a start-up can be scary. In this chapter, we embraced the big picture. We recapped the process of starting a blog business from mindset to completion.

YOUR QUICK START ACTION STEP:

Grasping the big picture can be scary, seeing as how your start-up is brand new. In the same way, we went about brainstorming to discover your niche, this would be a great time to take a breath. Let's brainstorm some ways you can keep motivated as you roll out your blog over the coming months and years.

1. What *is* your big picture? Your long-term plan? Fundamentally and ideally, what do you want your blog to accomplish for you? Personally? Professionally?

2. Consider whether, depending on your niche, your blog is a solo endeavor. Do you intend to hire writers and staff? If so, how will you recruit them?

3. Do you have a goal for your monthly earnings? Just because this book is subtitled "How to Make Money Blogging and Earn Up to $10,000 a Month" doesn't mean you need to aspire to that ceiling.

4. Now write down a list of strategies that you can use to keep motivated in the long run. Scheduling posts and maintaining a calendar so that you show your audience that you are consistent is only half the battle. How are you going to produce content regularly? How are you going to find new topics to discuss in your sub-niches?

5. Finally, identify a dozen or so sub-niches if your blog expands. If your initial niche is too narrow, now would be the perfect time to think about how to make your blog modular.

BONUS Chapter: Integrating Social Media

BONUS Chapter: Integrating Social Media

Some people believe that web marketing is all about tweaking code. Others preach the virtues of social networking. To boost web traffic to your site, you should explore one or both techniques.

In this chapter, we will take a brief look at how to integrate social media into your WordPress blog. Then we will dabble in rich media. Neither social media nor rich media are essential components of a successful blog business. But both could play a pivotal role in raising your blog above the average.

The social media universe is big, and it's expanding. Some of the more popular social media hubs include:

- Facebook
- Twitter
- YouTube
- Google+
- LinkedIn

Social media links are usually located either in the footer or in a sidebar widget. Choose whichever option looks best with your theme and your strategy for social media integration. That is, if social media is important to you and you expect to be tweeting on a regular basis, for example, make sure your link to Twitter is visible and easily findable on your blog.

As is usually the case with social media, and with blogging in general, one thing to remember is that readers don't want to be overwhelmed by too many options.

Loading your blog with unnecessary fluff will distract and turn off your audience. Stated another way, be discriminating about which social media hubs you decide to use. If you think generating blog content in the form of posts is time-consuming, maintaining a social media presence on one or more networks is infinitely more time-consuming. Choose only the networks that you currently use.

*Note: Another thing you might want to consider is if your niche market has its own go-to social media network. For example, my hypothetical DoggieLove101.com links to Rover.com, where my readers can connect with dog walkers and pet sitters.

WordPress also comes loaded with features that you can use for the same purposes as these social media sites.

- Comments
- RSS (really simple syndication)

The comments feature in WordPress is robust and customizable. If you are concerned about spam on your site, the comments feature can simply be turned off altogether. But if you are committed to welcoming your readers to contribute and talk back to your individual posts, comments are the way to do it! Comments on WordPress allow you to interact with your audience on an individual basis. It's a great way to start a conversation.

RSS (really simple syndication) feeds can be used in the same way as newsletters or email updates to keep your audience informed about updates on your blog. RSS feeds can also be a great feature to use to show your readers that you are an active and energetic blogger.

Social Networking and Facebook

Facebook was launched in 2004 by Mark Zuckerberg. Today, it has over 2 billion active users. It was the first really successful social networking site after MySpace and Friendster. In addition to personal profiles, organizations and businesses can have a presence on Facebook in the form of pages (as opposed to profiles). Facebook pages give companies and users a place to interact. Businesses can post updates and news on their Facebook page, respond to customer comments or inquiries, and integrate media via

Instagram and chat instantly with Messenger. On Facebook, you can build a following much easier

Facebook is a great place to go to build a following. With features such as the "like" button and following, it allows you to track and gauge your audience while also generating new traffic. Facebook and WordPress can be integrated pretty easily. You can place a Facebook icon on your blog, and then place a link to your blog on your Facebook page. We will take a closer look at how to do that in the quick steps at the end of this chapter.

Microblogging and Twitter

Twitter, along with Facebook, are two of the most popular social networking sites on the Web. Twitter was founded in 2006. Today, Twitter has over 300 million active users. It is what's known as a microblogging site. Users post "tweets" composed of less than 140 characters. The character limit was doubled in 2017. Tweets appear on your profile page in reverse chronological order.

Even though a blog and a microblog might sound a lot alike, it's not uncommon to see WordPress and Twitter being used simultaneously. There are a lot of things that you can do on Twitter that you can't on WordPress and vice versa. New blog posts can be auto tweeted to reach a broader community. Twitter can be integrated into WordPress in order to either link to your profile or display your twitter feed.

Like Facebook and the blogosphere, Twitter is an online community. Users can communicate with each other via twitter using hashtags (i.e., #Yoga4Life). Like Facebook, Twitter users can be followed by others, and tweets can be "liked."

Vlogging and YouTube

Vlogging (short for video blogging) is much newer and slightly less known than blogging. That being said, it's a lot more fun and a lot flashier. It's hard to say when vlogging first started, but it became popular around 2005. Vloggers can use an online video platform such as YouTube or Vimeo to host their videos. Vloggers can also link or embed their videos in WordPress.

Vloggers post videos the same way bloggers write posts. One common strategy is to record first person testimonials in which the vlogger speaks directly to the camera as if he or she were personally addressing the audience.

Even if you do not intend to launch a vlog, you should at least consider some sort of rich media integration for your blog. A blog that consists only of text can be boring and not visually appealing. Adding images, videos, and other interactive features like widgets increases the appeal of your site and will encourage visitors to remain on your site for longer durations.

You could consider linking to videos

made by others that relate to your blog post topic, adding photos or images to a blog post, or linking to music of podcasts that explore the topic of your post. For instance, when while composing a post for DoggieLove101.blog, our hypothetical blogger decides that she wants to show her readers how to trim a dog's nails. It's much more interesting and informative than reading about it. She will follow these steps to insert a video into her blog post.

If you decide to shoot the video yourself, the process is pretty straight forward.

1. Vloggers often use webcams, but camera phones work too. You don't need to have professional video equipment to be a vlogger.

2. Shoot and edit the video.
3. Upload the video to YouTube
4. Embed the video on your blog.
5. Once the video has uploaded, navigate to the page.
6. Click "Share"
7. Click "Embed."
8. In the popup window, copy the HTML code.
9. On your blog, open your post.
10. Toggle to the HTML tab.
11. Place your cursor at the location where you want your video to display.
12. Paste the embed code.
13. Toggle back to the visual tab to adjust alignment, if necessary.
14. You're done! Remember to publish or republish the post.

If you decide to borrow someone else's

video, the process is a little trickier. You will either need to have the filmmaker's consent, or else find a relevant video that has been published under a license that allows for reuse for commercial purposes.

1. Go to search.creativecommons.org.
2. Click the option for "use for commercial purposes"
3. Now, click the "YouTube" button.
4. Type your search terms into the text field.
5. Click the "Search" button.
6. Creative commons will redirect you to YouTube
7. YouTube will display in the SERP a list of relevant videos that have been published under the

Creative Commons Attribution license.

8. That means, these videos are as good as in the public domain. You can modify and adapt the content, and you are free to use it to promote your products on your blog.

9. Complete the process of embedding the video in your WordPress post by following steps 6-14 above.

*Note: There are lots of types of "media" (or mediums). Social media and rich media, for instance, are both forms of communication. Social media refers specifically to online and other interactive technologies that facilitate social networking. Examples include Facebook and Twitter. Rich media, on the other hand, refers to moving or still images and/or sounds. Examples include video, podcasts, sound files, and photographs. Both types of media add visual appeal to a blog.

More Resources

This chapter mentioned several of the more popular social media sites and interactive tools built into WordPress. As stated at the start of the chapter, the social media universe is wide. Here are some other networks that you might consider integrating into your blog business by a niche market.

General

- about.me
- Foursquare

For education

- Academia.edu
- Classmates.com
- Ratemyprofessors.com

Rich media

- Hulu
- Flickr
- Instagram

Travel

- Couchsurfing
- Hospitality Club
- Airbnb
- Meetup

Arts and Music

- DeviantArt
- Last.fm
- SoundCloud

CHAPTER SUMMARY:

In this bonus chapter, we took a quick look at some tools that you can use to enhance the visual and interactive design of your blog. Be discriminating about which tools you choose, and how you integrate them into your WordPress theme. Too much can be overwhelming. A lack of content on the social media site to which you link will turn off potential readers.

YOUR QUICK START ACTION STEP:

We discussed widgets in chapter 7 when we walked through the steps to add a HopLink to your blog. In this lesson, we will add a new widget to your blog. This widget will display your social media links.

1. Log into WordPress.

2. From your dashboard, go to Customize.

3. In the navigation bar, click Widgets.

4. Different themes support widgets in different areas of the page. Depending on your theme, widgets might be located in the header, in the footer, or in the left or right sidebars.

5. Choose which area you would like to display your social media links in.

6. Click "Add Widget".

7. Click on the widget called "Social Icons."

8. The Widget is automatically entitled "Follow Us," but you can change the title to whatever you want.

9. Choose what size you want the widget to appear in, small, medium, or large.
10. Add as many icons you want: Facebook, Twitter, YouTube, etc.
11. Copy and paste the link from your social media site into the text box entitled "account".
12. WordPress will display the icon of the social media network in the widget.
13. When a user clicks on the widget, they will be redirected to your page on the social media site.
14. Tip: Don't overload it. Only link to the social media platforms on which you intend to use frequently.

Conclusion

Thank you again for owning this book!

I hope that, with this book, you will be able to open doors through which you can further explore blogging and Affiliate marketing. The ultimate goal of this book is and has been to open up a path for you to learn more about how to use web-based blogging platforms to earn passive income. We hope that the steps provided in these chapters will help you discover a path toward earning an income with blogging with Affiliate marketing.

The next step is to continue to build your site. Continue to explore plugins, themes, customization options, and Social Media. As you develop your voice as a blogger, you will also continue to build upon the knowledge you already hold as a passionate aficionado of the niche market of your choice.

And, as you continue to accumulate blog

posts, expand your repertoire of categories, and develop a loyal readership, continue to remind yourself that blogging is a business. Readers are analogous to consumers.

Don't forget about the careful dynamic balanced between your passion for your niche market and your business acumen. In developing an audience for your blog, it will be important for you to learn how to maintain a consistent voice in your blog posts. You are not actively selling your merchant's products. However, you need to remember that you are their advocate.

Thank you, and good luck!